ENJOYING
SEXUAL
BLISS
IN YOUR MARRIAGE

Dr. Olubusola Olufemi

THE
CORNERSTONE
PUBLISHING

ENJOYING SEXUAL BLISS IN YOUR MARRIAGE

Cornerstone Publishing

A Division of Cornerstone Creativity Group LLC
Phone: +1(516) 547-4999
info@thecornerstonepublishers.com
www.thecornerstonepublishers.com

To order bulk of this book or to contact the author for speaking engagement please email:

dro@femfiswellness.com

CONTENTS

DEDICATION

I dedicate this book to God for the power
of love, intimacy and friendship; and to the
memory of my parents, who showed me that
true love does exist.

ACKNOWLEDGMENTS

I thank God, the Almighty, who has made it possible for me to finally write this book. I thank Him for His work of grace and mercy in my life; I have seen His hand open doors of opportunities and provide the right resources, just at the right time. I appreciate Him for His inspiration, encouragement and affirmation when I needed it the most. I am humble for His call upon my life to proclaim His Good News.

There is a lot of work that goes into publishing and marketing a book that most people will never know. By the time you hold a copy of this book to read, it would have passed through many hands that made it a reality. I have so many people to thank for their immense contributions to this journey. So, I want to take this time to thank the many partners who have been so generous and instrumental to making this a reality.

First and foremost, I thank Pastor Gbenga Showunmi of Cornerstone Creativity & Publishing Group, for pushing me till the end. This work is a compilation of my notes of over ten years and I sincerely appreciate Alpsedge Associates, led by Funke Fasunon, for pulling it all together. My sincere thanks to Ayodeji Olobatuyi of Xpression Photos, for sowing the seed to push this book and for my beautiful portrait. My friend and sister, Evangelist Abiola Fashina, never stopped to push me since the first day we met, to publish a book. I kept promising her for the last four years and she kept pushing until this birth.

A big thank you to my administrative staff, Damilola Awe and Adedayo Sodeke, for their support always. Without you both, I would not be able to do many things. Sincere thanks to my Manager, Omolola Oluranti and staff, Tolulope Oluranti, for their sacrifice and help in achieving targets. My appreciation goes to Adedapo Adegoke and Shalewa Teniola for reviewing this book with me. God bless you both.

To my little sister, who is always concerned about me, Gbemisola Bankole; and my friend, Abiodun Akwe, I appreciate you both for your love. Pastor Brenda Ademoroti, Prophet Lewis Philips, thank you always for your intercessory prayers. God indeed answered your prayers. And to my Audacious Women of Purpose prayer line partners, God bless you all abundantly for your love, support and prayers all these years we have been together.

To all the wonderful friends and families that support and pray for me tirelessly, may God bless and honor you always. I pray for a special blessing upon my followers on Facebook and Instagram for their prayers, support and love. Without your openness and support for many years, this book would not have come to life. To everyone that has ever shared their lives, secrets, pains and struggles with me, thank you and may God continue to bless your lives.

I will always remain grateful to God for my husband, who continually shows himself as God's gift to me. God bless and favor you always, Stephen Olufemi. You have truly shown me the color of love, intimacy and commitment. A special thank you to my wonderful children for their love, encouragement and patience. You always give me the support to go and achieve whatever my mind desires. I love you all for your understanding and I pray that, together, we will continue to serve God as a family.

To everyone that will open and read the pages of this book, I pray that you experience the unconditional love of God, and may your life be beautiful.

PREFACE

The wedding was expectedly spectacular, but the honeymoon was something else. Let's just say it was a letdown – the result of the baggage of misconceptions that both had refused to drop at the door. And so, the honeymoon that was meant to be the climax of the wedding, turned out to be the anti-climax, with the air of mutual dissatisfaction clouding the room.

On the first night, both had blamed fatigue for the other's attitude, but after a few days, an uneasy doubt began to creep in, precipitating the all-too-familiar misgiving: "Oh no, is she really like that?" "Can he be so naïve?" Soon, the doubts began to take on a semblance of reality. Few months down the road, both could only wake up and think, "What in the world have I done?"

The above scenario is much more familiar than you may think. I hear stories every day and they are authentic. Often, when people realize that life will not be a fairy tale after all, they become confused. To deal with this, many simply lower their expectations and close their mouths most of the time. Some others choose to run their mouths more than usual or just try to make the best of things. Still, much of the frustration remains. They repress it as long and as hard as they can, but from time to time, those little annoying things their spouses do become like matches thrown into a barrel of gasoline (not pretty at all). Yes, it gets fiery sometimes and mostly it is all about sex.

Indeed, in the midst of the crises that daily convulse our world, the most intimate and dangerous war is the war that goes on in our homes - the fact that we cannot make peace in our kitchens or bedrooms, and the fact that we cannot make peace in our hearts with the ones we supposedly love. The good news, however, is that there is a way out. We can let go and create a new beginning. We can steadily transit from the depths of bickering and boredom in our homes to the heights of blessedness and bliss!

I have been inspired to write this book because I see a crisis that needs attention and someone has got to do the job. I am a very practical person. I work and deal with real people, with real issues and struggles, and I learn from their mistakes and their victories. My purpose here is not to offer bandages for all the wounds or grievances we have in our marriages and bedrooms. My purpose is to address the major challenges we are having so that we can make our marital life as exciting and enriching as God desires it to be.

The expositions in this book are to guide you through the process of seeing things differently and ultimately enjoying better and more fulfilling intimacy in your marriage. The point is for you to use what you already know and what you discover here to begin an all-encompassing process of transformation. Hope is what enables us to face tomorrow with anticipation and joy. Don't give up yet; there is hope. God can turn your marriage into something that resembles heaven on earth!

CHAPTER 1

MADE FOR YOUR PLEASURE

"Sex isn't something sinful, but rather a wonderful gift from God to be thoroughly enjoyed within the boundaries of marriage"

— Ray Comfort

Sex is one of the most profound gifts of God to mankind. It is, in fact, the most powerful and pleasurable passion He ever created. And I daresay that it is the clearest pointer to His special interest in the marriage institution — since it is a gift that He expects to be unlocked only as soon as a man and a woman are joined together in holy matrimony. Not only does this reveal the exceptional premium He places on the marital union but it also confirms the sacredness and significance of sexual intimacy in His agenda for the human race.

All of God's gifts are good and perfect. And these include sex. It is thus impossible for God to give a "dirty", "distasteful" or "shameful" gift as many people have come to see sex. I will shortly be detailing the many benefits of sexual intimacy or frequent lovemaking in marriage, but let me quickly call your attention to the fact that parents are usually eager to provide their children who are getting married with gifts that they know will be of the greatest delight and benefit to them. How much more the Almighty God who knows the end from the beginning! As soon as He conducted the first wedding between the first man and woman, He gave them (and their descendants that would follow after them) the drive and license of lovemaking, saying: "Therefore a man shall leave his father and mother and be joined to his wife, and they shall become one flesh" (Genesis 2:24).

Did you notice that He doesn't say that they two shall "procreate"? No. Even though procreation is one of the fundamental purposes of marriage, it is not stated as the number one reason. The number one reason, as stated by God Himself, is for the man and the woman to bond and blend into each other in holy intimacy. And the immediate and most powerful "glue" He provided to make this work is the gift of sex. This means that sex, in its most elemental form, was God's idea and He intended it to be one of the most fulfilling activities in a couple's relationship.

Essentially, God's original blueprint for mankind is for marriage to be immensely pleasurable and it should cement the two individuals as "one flesh." Now, if God's primary purpose for marriage is that the couple must first become supernaturally bonded, it should be clear why he considers sex as the most important gift for the couple. Only through sexual intimacy can a couple fully know each other, without any reservations or pretensions. Both are laid bare before the other as they truly are and they are able to reach such level of knowledge about each other that no one else is expected to ever know.

It is not surprising that the verb often used in the Old Testament Scripture for couples engaging in sexual intimacy is "to know". Of course, a couple can know each other by communicating, interacting and spending quality time together. However, making love or having sex is the ultimate confirmation and consummation of this intimacy. Even in legal parlance, it is believed that to enforce a marriage, a couple has to "consummate" it by having sex soon after the wedding. It would seem then that without this confirmation, the covenant of a lasting bond cannot be said to have been established by couple. In the words of Sheila Gregoire, a Christian marriage expert, "Sex is meant to be a cornerstone of marriage. It isn't optional. When we let sex go, we're not just rejecting sex. We're rejecting that ultimate "knowing" of our spouse."

The implication is that the act of lovemaking between a couple transcends the physical act and has serious implications for spiritual and emotional bonding. This means that as long as a couple engages in the act, they perform a symbolic gluing of their lives together and thereby reinforcing God's purpose for the marriage institution and positioning themselves for unstoppable exploits and blessings!

Is Sex Overhyped?

It is not uncommon to hear people say that sex is overrated or overhyped. And, of course, they may seem right - because the scope of sex and human sexuality has, in recent times, been pushed beyond acceptable limits by satanic agents. We live in a sex-saturated culture. The world and the devil have attempted to make the subject of sex their domain. Everywhere we look, we see seductive images and hear titillating words. It is in our faces everywhere, on the billboards, in the news, at checkpoints, on the internet. You do not have to ask for it, it is there, unsolicited, and when you take a second look, it might dominate your thoughts afterwards.

This is why I won't be surprised if there are people who, by merely seeing the title of this book, would simply let out an irritated sigh, roll their eyes, and dismiss it with an "here we go again..." scoff. It is even possible that you are reading it now with an indifferent attitude and waiting for the right moment to dump it. But let me tell you this. Nothing that comes from God and is used in the right way can be overrated. Proverbs 10:22 says, "The blessing of the Lord makes one rich, and He adds no sorrow with it." Every blessing from God is ever enriching and uplifting because it is a reflection of God the giver Himself. And since sex is a blessing from God, it goes without saying that it was never designed to evoke feelings of disgust, dread or disappointment but of ecstasy and fulfilment. It is meant to be enjoyed, not endured.

Shades of Sex

Reading through the feedback section of an online article on sex, I stumbled on a comment that said, "Sex is so overrated and endlessly talked about that it's becoming an exceptionally boring topic of conversation." What I found more interesting however was the response of another reader to this comment. It said, *"Sex is not overrated...you just ain't doing it right."*

I consider that response epic because it is so true. Sex that seems overrated, hollow and disillusioning has to be considered within the context of who is doing it and how it is being done. Such sex often falls into one or more of three categories. The first is one that is abused, misused and perverted. To abuse, misuse or pervert something is to use it for a wrong purpose or under the wrong circumstances. In the case of sex, it becomes perverted and ultimately feels overhyped when it is driven by pure lust.

All forms of illicit or immoral sex – that is, sex outside of marriage - fall under this category. Regardless of the hype in movies and the media in general, sex that is done outside of marriage often feels disappointing sooner or later because it is an abuse and misuse. King Solomon definitely had a firsthand experience in this. No wonder he wrote, "Food gained by fraud tastes sweet, but one ends up with a mouth full of gravel." (Proverbs 20:17). This, exactly, is true of sex. It begins to feel more like a poisonous, rather than a pleasurable experience when it is used by people for whom it was not designed.

Recently, I read the account of someone who had this disappointing experience with sex. And of course, I wasn't surprised at all, judging by the motive with which the individual approached sex in the first place. Here is her account:

> *"When I was a teenager, one of the hottest sex scenes I'd ever seen was in a movie. It spoke to every single fantasy I had about what sex was supposed to be – raw, sweaty, primal, wet, romantic, mind-blowing, perfect, effortless, hot, surrounded by candles, with flawless bodies, and ending in sweet laughter. This was what real sex was supposed to be. It's what Cosmo was telling me. When I finally did have sex for the first time…Sex, compared to the fantasy, was pretty disappointing. There was a feeling that sex is overrated."*

While some of the ideas that this individual had about sex were true, it's obvious that her understanding was grounded in utter distortion or perversion of the purpose of sex. You may have noticed that both the narrator and her various sources of information weren't discussing sexual intimacy in its default habitat – the marriage institution. It's all about lust and passion. And naturally, it didn't yield the sweetness and satisfaction she was expecting.

This is very instructive. When someone's goal is to abuse sex or when their expectations about sexual intimacy are based on the views and experiences of those who misuse sex, such as characters in movies and books or even porn stars, then they're bound to find sex deeply unfulfilling.

The second context in which sex can seem overhyped is when it is done in gross ignorance. Many times, people enter the marital union without much understanding of the uniqueness and differences between male and female sexualities. Some people do not even have a basic understanding of their own sexuality or how their body functions, much less that of their spouse. This ignorance can pose a major problem to their sexual life. A man, who, for instance, doesn't understand the importance of foreplay and decoding the signals from his wife's body could make sex a painful experience for her and a frustrating experience for himself. Similarly, a woman who doesn't understand that sex is about giving and taking, as well as understanding and communicating her feelings, might just lie down there, waiting for her husband to singlehandedly take her to the peak of bliss. In the end, they both feel dissatisfied and may consider sex to be overrated because they both do not understand the language or the act.

The joys of sex can also feel exaggerated when the act is done with certain emotional or psychological inhibitions. These inhibitions could stem from revolting notions about sex that have been instilled by their parents, guardians or religious community. Sometimes, in a bid to shield their children or wards from the snares of premarital sex, older people portray sex as a sinful, dirty or shameful act – and thus end up throwing the baby away with the bathwater. Unfortunately, while this approach may indeed achieve the primary objective of keeping the children away from immoral sex, the unpleasant images of sex sometimes get so entrenched in such children right into adulthood and inevitably infiltrate their marital life. Since sex has been painted evil and dirty, they continue to detest or merely tolerate it.

Emotional and psychological inhibitions about sex could also be offshoots of past traumatic sexual experiences, such as rape or assault, or dissatisfying sexual encounters with previous partners or present spouse. Haunting memories of these unpleasant experiences can dampen excitement in each subsequent act of lovemaking,

making sex become an endless cycle of burden to be endured.

With the baggage of misconceptions or exaggerated beliefs, or past unpleasant or embarrassing sexual experiences floating in someone's head, it becomes very difficult for them to let go of themselves and just enjoy the moment – a critical factor in enjoying awesome sex. Consequently, the person may end up reinforcing the notion in themselves that the joy of sex is simply being overhyped.

The True Picture

What you must understand about sexual intimacy, however, is that none of the negative scenarios above is in God's agenda for your life. God's purpose for you is to live your years in prosperity and pleasures (Job 36:11). And one of the means of achieving this in marriage is through sex – for sex, done God's way and with adequate knowledge, is about the most pleasurable physical activity you can engage in. This is why it is also very addictive.

Don't let anyone or any personal issue give you a negative impression about sex. God made us sexual beings and placed within us the capacity to enjoy a healthy, physical bonding relationship. He does not prevent it – we do! Let me emphasize it again. Sex is God-given. And it is his desire that all couples take back this sacred ground and enjoy this holy gift.

So, look at it again. If sex weren't so pleasurable, why has it become such a great attraction in our society, such that "sex sells" has become a popular slogan in the marketing, advertising and entertainment industries? Why have some people built multi-billion dollar empires on sexual perversions? Why do you think movies with steamy sex scenes and books on sexual fantasies often become bestsellers and blockbusters? And, most importantly, why do you think some people go to such extreme lengths of risking their lives, positions, reputations, peace of mind or losing so much of their monies to get a few minutes of the stolen pleasures of illicit sex? We even frequently hear cases of women who keep returning to their abusive boyfriends, simply because of sex. If those who pervert sex get such momentary high from it, how much more someone to whom it has been given as a gift to perpetually enjoy!

It is my desire that whatever it is that may have made sex become so distasteful to you will be rooted out of your life and relationship. This is exactly why we are going through this together and I can assure you that your sex life is about to experience a total makeover, such that you will not be able to get enough of this gift with your spouse!

Sex is not a Taboo

Men and women may have differing hopes about sex, but it is one of the most powerful forces in human nature.

Some couples talk openly about their desires, pleasure zones, creative positions, and problems related to their sex lives. For many others, however, this is a strenuous task. Often, due to certain factors having to do with their religious or cultural upbringing, many couples talk with each other about anything and everything except their sex lives. Their partners have to guess what their desires might be, and they can only hope they connect emotionally and physically to make it worth the effort. Sexual hopes and dreams are completely normal, and so are struggles in this area of our lives.

Really, many of us have made sex to be what it is not. Instead of it being fulfilling and fun, it feels seductive, manipulative and empty. And some of us grew up in families where sex was simply never mentioned. Everybody knew it happened occasionally, but it was a taboo subject. You can only imagine what might be going on behind closed doors. Our silence about the subject is following the example of our parents, and we are modeling the same thing to our kids. (I am talking to my kids now, using the age-appropriate approach).

Sometime ago, I went to speak with a bunch of sixth graders on the invitation of their teacher who had been so concerned about some of them. I met Ms. Smart (not real name) in a library while working on a new curriculum, "Creating Positive Relationships". She asked an adult question and we kept talking for a very long time. Then, she asked if I could simplify the curriculum

I was working on for youths as well. That was a big challenge but I love challenges!

Two months later, I called Ms. Smart to see what I had put together for her students. She was so excited she wanted me to share it as soon as was practically possible. Well, Valentine's Day was around the corner and what could be a perfect day to talk about love!

To say that I was shocked about some of the issues raised by these youngsters is to put it mildly! The seriousness of the encounter can only be understood in light of how fast these kids are growing, swamped at such an early age by sexuality that defies even conventional wisdom. Of course, we had a great time and I kept wishing I had someone to give me such lessons when I was 11 years old.

My point here is that it is very much okay to talk about sex. Come to think of it, can we truly deny the possibility of real sex-talk among young people and their peers in this sex-crazed world of ours today? The truth is that if you do not talk about it yourself, someone else will do it for you. As a parent, it is your duty to talk to your children about sex. Talk appropriately according to the age. You can simplify what sex is to a seven-year-old and be a little detailed to a teenager. What we need is simply a healthy balance to get it done!

The Church Factor

I have also discovered that most churches do not talk about sex at all and even when they do, it is so vague and monotonous, making many Christians feel embarrassed by the subject. Yet, we think about it and fantasize about it. In fact, our hearts bleed because of it and we remain miserable for it. Worse is that because it is mostly portrayed as a forbidden subject, many church-goers have come to believe that it is somehow not on the list of God's best gifts.

Inside the pages of our Bibles, we find the intriguing and racy little book of the Song of Solomon; it seems to describe passionate lovemaking (see Song of Solomon 4:1-7, 5:11-16 and 8:3-4, 13-14). Do not be deceived; the open, loving and joyful expression of sexual desire in marriage is good and godly. The thrills we enjoy with our spouse fulfill our marriage vows to become one. God does not scowl at us when we plan creative sexual encounters with our spouse, and He does not frown when we actually enjoy ourselves. He delights in us enjoying the good gifts He has given us.

I have not seen a single verse in the Bible that describes sex as sinful, dirty, or wrong. Just as I noted before, sex only becomes sinful when it is experienced outside a loving, intimate commitment between a husband and a wife. That is what the Bible speaks against! Sex, as God intended, is a beautiful thing. So why set a limit on it?

I honestly cannot fathom why the church treats sex as a taboo subject. We do not want to talk about it but many church people do it, even outside of their marriages. They sneak around, thinking, wishing, surfing, soliciting and fantasizing, just to feel high and gratify their desires. We all know of families or marriages in crisis but what are we doing about it? We would rather raise funds for church anniversaries than organize a marriage seminar and invite a professional to come and speak to the congregation.

A Pastor called me recently to ask a question and we talked at length. At the end of it all, he asked if I could come to his church to sing (I was a choir director for some years). He would rather let me do the worship than talk to the congregation about the same question that he had just asked me—sex in marriage. He said we couldn't talk about that in the church. No wonder we always have sex scandals in our churches. We just do not get our priorities right, do we?

If sex is God's invention, why can we not talk about it in our churches? Do a very serious anonymous survey in your church and truthfully see how many couples are truly happy about their sex life. We just do not get it. We need to invest in our marriages more than we invest in other things that are not as important. Can you be a Christian and still be sensuous? Yes, you bet, and very well indeed!

We can organize parties at club meetings and town meetings and bring in all the celebrity Pastors and singers. No wonder the church is full of single parents, separated and divorced couples. We have a crisis going on and I personally think it is about time we do something about it. If I sound too harsh, it is because I deal with this on a daily basis and I know things could be better; we just need to pay more attention and invest in our marriages.

Let's begin to see sex the way God wants us to see it. Sex is not just for procreation; it is the tango of the soul for married couples. It is joyous and is a time of giving and sharing. It is tender and holy and should be as natural as drinking a glass of water.

Sex was never meant to be a single act of expression or feeling. On the contrary, gentleness, understanding, acts of kindness, and self-sacrifice all combine to become the building blocks of sexual satisfaction. Sex is about joining with your partner as God designed, for warmth, intimacy, and bonding. Sex is a divine symphony between two lovers, and God is leading the orchestra, it should be a beautiful experience!

CHAPTER 2

THE JOYS OF SEX

"Done well, marital sexuality can be a supremely healing experience."

— Gary L. Thomas

So, what's really special about sex and why should you be having it as much as possible? I mentioned in the previous chapter that it was not accidental that the very first gift that God gave the first couple was the license to make love. This, I'm sure, is because of the amazing benefits He has embedded in the act.

The truth is that God has wired us for sex from the very beginning and the fact that He created some parts of our body to exclusively provide and respond to sexual sensations shows that He purposely designed sex to be a truly thrilling experience and not just for making babies.

However beyond the ecstatic feelings that come with making love is the avalanche of emotional, psychological, health and spiritual rejuvenation attached to it.

Lovemaking has been designed by God to enhance your quality of life, as well as that of your spouse and your marriage in unimaginable ways. To begin with, more than anything else, sex strengthens and solidifies the emotional bond between you and your spouse. In fact, someone aptly describes it as the "atomic bond that holds a marriage together."

This indeed is one of the wonders that God has wired into lovemaking. It creates an inexplicable connection that is often difficult to dissolve. It is rare for couples who make love often not to have a strong bond with each other, just as it is difficult for couples who rarely make love not to feel a sense of disconnect from each other.

It may interest you to know that, in addition to the spiritual perspective on the bonding power of sex, there are scientific proofs to show that sex truly strengthens a marriage relationship and creates deeper intimacy between couples. Before going into the science of sex, however, let me say that I think one of the reasons sex strengthens a marriage is that God has done it in such a way that the sublime feelings that come with sex easily override the negative feelings of stress, lethargy, irritation, resentment and even sorrow and grief – all of which have the potential to weaken the structure of a marriage.

Even for people who are not married, once sex comes into the picture, it becomes so easy to overlook offences and other disagreeable character traits. In fact, sex often tends to cover a multitudes of evils – even if temporarily. How many times do people wonder why a nice, decent lady remains hooked to a man who seems irresponsible and hardly respects her? This is why premarital sex is often discouraged, especially for those in courtship. It is because people who frequently have sex hardly find time to critically analyze vital issues relating to their relationship – especially if such issues have the potential of causing disagreement. Sex simply covers it all – until they get married and eventually realize that, while sex is indeed an awesome experience, it cannot meet all marital needs.

This addicting and bonding power of sex is not just another proof that God only intended sexual intimacy for married people but also shows that He originally planned that sex should be a beautiful and crucial part of the marital union for the couple to remain continually joined together according to His plan. "Sex," says Andy Stanley, "is a bit like glue. You shouldn't apply it until you are sure you want to stick two things together permanently." Yes, sex works!

Scientific Angle

Studies from various fields of human endeavor have, at different times, scientifically proven that lovemaking is a phenomenal act that involves a sequence of physical, biological and psychological processes which combine to create a most blissful and bonding experience for the couple. Pepper Schwartz, PhD, a professor of sociology at the University of Washington in Seattle, explained that sexual attraction and sexual arousal bring to bear two very important hormones, dopamine and oxytocin, both of which create bliss and bonding.

"Even if the lovemaking session started out with only a modest amount of interest, once arousal starts, these hormones create attachment, pleasure, and intimacy," she said, adding that "frequent sex is a great bonus and even an essential part of most couple's commitment and happiness with one another."

True to Schwartz's findings and those of others, during lovemaking, a cocktail of feel-good hormones are released throughout our bodies, lighting up the reward centers in our brains. The two most powerful of these hormones - oxytocin and dopamine (also known as love hormones) - have been known to have magical effects on the human brain. When we make love, these two chemicals work in dynamic ways to create links between our neural systems which produce uncommon endearment between us and our spouses.

Produced in the hypothalamus, oxytocin, also called "cuddle hormone", floods our brain with a soothing feeling of happiness and empathy, which makes us to easily lower our defenses and trust our partner the more. This relationship-building hormone, which is also involved during childbirth and breastfeeding, comes with a surge during lovemaking. With the rush of oxytocin in the brain, nothing else matters to a couple anymore, other than the desire to be with each other.

Dopamine acts in a similar way as oxytocin. However, while oxytocin is the bonding hormone, dopamine is the pleasure or "bliss" hormone. It is what makes sex feels so good. During lovemaking, it fills us with uncommon excitement and euphoria. That's where the mind-blowing and addicting feeling comes from, and together with the bonding feeling from oxytocin, it is easy to see why frequent lovemaking should have such sustaining power in a relationship.

Naturally, then, to strengthen the marital bond, oxytocin and dopamine levels need to be kept high. And while these hormones can be released in limited amounts through some other pleasurable activities that couples may engage in individually and collectively, it is through lovemaking that they are best unleashed.

Practical Demonstration

Most couples in a loving relationship can readily attest

to the magical effect of sex in deepening their intimacy. But in case you are still not fully convinced by the above insights, I'm delighted to let you know that there are documented records of couples who actually set out to see whether improving their sex lives could improve their relationship, and their discoveries are astonishing.

Some years back, a couple, Brad and Charla Muller, decided to reignite the passion in their eight-year-old marriage, by choosing to have sex every day for one year. You might have heard of this story. It was actually Charla's idea, as she felt that the connection between her and her husband wasn't as strong as it used to be in the early years of their marriage – before the kids and other commitments got in the way. So, as a way of celebrating Brad's 40th birthday, she suggested that they had sex every day for a whole year. After some initial hesitation, he agreed. And even though it wasn't an easy commitment for the couple, what they realized eventually was that the sacrifice was worth it.

Indeed, so impressive was the transformation that came to their marriage and life in general that Charla documented the experience in a book, 365 Nights: *A Memoir of Intimacy*. According to her, "I didn't realize how much not being intimate stressed our relationship… Nowadays we're much more relaxed with each other and the house isn't full of unspoken tension…It was partly a challenge to see if we could do that every day for a year. And we proved we could. Now we're reaping the benefits. Before, sex was abysmal. Now I have discovered I do have time for quality sex on a regular basis, which wasn't what was happening before. So, now, intimacy - and that includes sex - is better than it's ever been."

Just like Charla and Brad, another couple, Douglas and Annie Brown, also decided to try rekindling intimacy in their marriage of 14 years by having sex every day for 101 days. Again, the result, as Douglas documented in his book, *Just Do It: How One Couple Turned Off the TV and Turned On Their Sex Lives for 101 Days,* was explosive. He revealed that frequent lovemaking released "an avalanche" of pleasures upon their marriage. In His words, "We learned so much about each other. Sex became much more playful and that translated into a more playful union. We regained electricity that wasn't always there before."

I have shown you these examples, not with the intention of asking you to have sex daily, but to let you know that sex works miracles in a marriage – and that's exactly what God designed it for!

Beyond Intimacy

However, beyond the passion and intimacy that sex adds to marriage, people like the above couples and many more can also confirm that having sex frequently will make a couple happier, less angry, and less stressed.

Charla, whose experience I shared above, also said of her marriage: "Regular sex was allowing for feelings of health and wellness that sparked a desire to have more sex. Sex is a great stress-reliever too. A nice relaxing romp with Brad was a wonderful distraction from feeling like the world would crumble if I wasn't out there battling dragons 24/7. I could relax, feel those endorphins pinging around my body and forget about my bad day. And perhaps best of all, our intimate moments were making me feel younger."

Corroborating this, Helen Fisher, PhD, a research professor at Rutgers University, said, "Sex is designed to make you feel good for a reason. With someone you love, I recommend it for many reasons: It's good for your health and good for your relationship. It's good for respiration, muscles, and bladder control. It's a fine antidepressant, and it can renew your energy."

So, in view of the above, I have compiled below a few fascinating facts on the benefits of sex that you will find interesting:

10 Fascinating Facts about Sex

- Sex is good exercise. Every time you make love, you burn between 100 and 150 calories. That is as many calories as you will burn in a brisk twenty-minute walk!

- Sex is good medicine. Studies indicate that women's

pain thresholds rise during sexual activity. This means chronic conditions like arthritis, low-back pain, and even PMS may be helped.

- Sex improves your skin tone and color by increasing blood flow and helping your skin to regenerate and become more pliable and elastic. In other words, sex makes your skin supple and radiant. You simply GLOW!

- Sex stimulates endorphin release, which enables you to sleep more soundly like a baby.

- Sex is a great cardiovascular workout. During sex, the heart rate may reach 130 beats a minute.

- Sex is a natural antidepressant. It boosts your mood and reduces irritability or crankiness, trust me, depression can not knock on your door.

- Sex reduces the chances of some cancers, such as cancer of the prostate. Have great sex and your balls will be healthy for it.

- Sex enhances your brainpower with better cognitive function and the growth of new brain cells.

- Sex boosts your immunity to ward off certain infections, like common cold and flu.

- Sex can help you get regular periods and reduce cramps.

So, what are you waiting for? Sex is God's gift to you and your spouse and you can enjoy it for as long as you want and get all the goodies it has to offer. No restrictions. No inhibitions. No limits. Just do it!

CHAPTER 3

CATALYST OF INTIMACY

"If we're not intentional about pursuing God's best for our marriages, and grasping the tremendous role intimacy plays in that relationship, what was intended to be deeply enjoyed - a passionate, life-giving love affair... alight with laughter, fiercely protected, and drenched in freedom - becomes a stuffy, awkward thing to be endured."

— Joy McMillan

Good sex begins with good intimacy. That's the simple truth. Sex doesn't begin with the act of lovemaking itself; it begins with all the little, thoughtful and tender ways in which we daily create an atmosphere of love, harmony, trust and emotional connection in the home. In fact, a primary reason the subject of sex sounds repulsive to many people is because the very thought of having sex with the person they share their lives with turns them off. It's like they are merely being forced to share their lives with a familiar stranger.

Lovemaking requires that a couple be in sync with each other and make themselves vulnerable. Once there is unresolved tension or a sense of disconnect between them, sex becomes a chore or even a punishment, rather than a pleasurable experience. Take a look again at that romantic book of the Bible – Song of Solomon. It says in 5:16, "This is my love, and this is my friend". What this means is that you cannot have a real and satisfying lovemaking experience if you cannot look at your spouse and say, "This is my friend!"

Someone rightly said that the best sex is not being had by people in the hookup culture but by people who are totally and completely comfortable with their spouses. That is the whole truth. Intimacy is, indeed, the best aphrodisiac. To give and receive good sex requires that both partners completely trust each other to be genuinely committed to their collective needs, wellbeing, happiness and satisfaction.

The Scripture says of Adam and Eve that, despite being naked, they were not ashamed of each other. The reason was that they saw themselves as one. There was perfect love which "casts out fear" between them, and so each could be comfortable with being bare before the other, without feeling exposed, coerced, cheated or taken for granted. Simply put, they were the best of soul-mates!

Connecting with Your Spouse's Soul

Connecting with the soul of your spouse begins with the understanding that intimacy is not a single, isolated act, such as a memorable and romantic dinner or a pleasurable sexual experience in an attractive room. Those are just stages in which intimacy might unfold. Intimacy is not an event; it's what happens during these events. Two people actively pursuing the other person's deepest being. It is speaking the language of the other person's soul. Becoming and staying engaged requires that you step outside of yourself and consider him or her just as supremely important and valuable as you are, even if their passivity drives you nuts.

In the end, the highpoint of intimacy is two souls risking vulnerability and weaving a life together that couldn't be made without the congealing of wills. It demands both humility and creativity. And it does not just happen; it has to be cultivated. Intimacy is not for the proud and the timid; the reward goes to the humble and the brave!

Intimacy is the action fuel that turns new love into deep love. It provides a level of closeness that love's infatuations alone cannot deliver. Intimacy, respect and other related blessings either grow or shrivel. They are fed, or they starve. The human heart grows heavier when burdened with the excruciating emotions and elements common to marriages. With romance alone, people enter in and exit; but with marriage, there is no easy or ready-made exit door from the arena into which two people voluntarily pledge, through remarkable promises, to join and devote their lives.

Here, two foreign souls interact, interrelate, and are expected to work things out through the turbulent waters of conflicts and resolutions, elements of intimacy that create unmatched closeness between two people. If we do not connect and share who we are with each other, then there is no relationship.

Love as the Bedrock of Intimacy

Intimacy, as has been noted, has to do with creating an atmosphere of love and trust. Love means different things to different people, and it is shown in different ways. The most common ways people want to be loved can range from quality time, words of affirmation and receiving gifts to acts of service and physical touch.

Most spouses I see in therapy long to be loved intimately; but they struggle with relationship discord, shame and control issues - anger, abuse and fears of abandonment - that block closeness and damage their sexual lives. It does not have to be this way, and I believe things can take a better turn, once we allow the love of God to flood our hearts and homes.

Love is, above all, the gift of oneself to the other person. I talk to people and hear about couples who live in loveless marriages – relationships of convenience – where the love has died or possibly never really existed in any substantial way, to begin with. These couples believe that their current situations are really as good as they will ever get, and they have no hope that anything will change. Let me quickly say that even though it is generally accepted that men and women see and experience love through very different lenses, I believe that all we need do sometimes is clean our lenses and see love in its purest form!

Here's what the Bible says on this in 1 John 4:7-12, 16, "Dear friends, let us love one another, for love comes from God. Everyone who loves has been born of God and knows God. Whoever does not love does not know God, because God is love. This is how God showed His love among us: He sent His one and only son into the world that we might live through him. This is love: not that we love God, but that He loved us and sent His son as an atoning sacrifice for our sins. Dear friends, since God so loved us, we also ought to love one another. No one has ever seen God; but if we love one another, God lives in us and His love is made complete in us...God is love. Whoever lives in love lives in God, and God in Him."

Christ gave His love, when it was not deserved, to people who did not deserve it. That is a principle you are going to have to practice in your marriage, if it is to be an exciting and lasting one. There will come times when you will need to give love to your spouse, love that is not deserved, and give it joyfully. We are all angels with one wing, and we need each other to fly. Marriage is God's idea, and it is the microcosm of heaven on earth. But the glue that holds it together is the unconditional love of God for one another. We all cry out for genuine love, love that heals, love that unites, love that forgives, love that encourages. Love is essential to our emotional, physical, mental, and social well-being. Our lives are shaped by those who love us and by those who refuse to love us.

God is able to create and stir a heart of love even in the loveless, just as He is able to make a saint out of a desperate and self-absorbed sinner. God can use you in this process. Good enough, the Scripture shows us exactly how we can show love to a loveless and difficult person. 1 Corinthians 13: 4-8 says, "Love is patient, love is kind. It does not envy, it does not boast, it is not proud. It is not rude, it is not self-seeking, it is not easily angered, it keeps no record of wrongs. Love does not delight in evil but rejoices with the truth. It always protects, always trusts, always hopes, always perseveres. Love never fails."

This gives us a clear picture of the kind of love God wants us to have and demonstrate to foster intimacy in our marriages. Such love is not envious or boastful, proud or rude, self-seeking, angry and unwilling to let go of wrongs, nor does it rejoice in evil. Rather, it is patient and kind (love is not in a hurry); it rejoices with the truth (love delights in the good things in life); it always protects (love wants what's best for the other person, no matter what the situation); it always trusts, hopes, and perseveres (love is everlasting)

Ultimately, love is an understanding and the mature acceptance of imperfection. It is real. It gives you strength and grows beyond you – to bolster your beloved. You are warmed by the presence of your beloved, even when they are away. Miles do not separate you. You want them nearer. But nearer or not, you know they are yours, and you can wait.

Love is the maturation of friendship. You must be friends before you can be lovers. We all know that there are significant, large-scale factors hindering the ignition of desire for intimacy; but don't be discouraged and don't give up before trying, because the good news is that all of these factors can be overcome. Fundamental differences between men and women make achieving intimacy a challenge in itself. However, with increased challenge comes greater character and greater reward. Know yourself, open your heart, share yourself, and the comfort of closeness with your spouse will follow. I am a living proof!

Making Intimacy Work

For the average woman, feeling emotionally close to your partner often inspires you to want to be sexual with him. For men, however, it is often the opposite. Most men usually need sex in order to feel emotionally close to their partner. In order for intimacy and sex to be successful in a relationship, women and men must work to understand what the other needs. Couples must work on feeling connected as a team in all areas of their lives. Your job is to ask for what you want and need in the relationship in order to keep the sexual fire burning in the long term.

As married couples, we all desire passion in our relationship, but with the pressures of careers, kids, and day-to-day commitments, we do not make time to create the fireworks. So, let me encourage you - just spice it up a little, unleash the baby inside and get in touch with some of your deeper desires and gently push yourself to move beyond the same old routine.

There are endless opportunities both inside and outside the bedroom for boosting your sensual power as a couple. Changing your routine restores novelty to your relationship. When I realized that my relationship with my husband had started to encounter challenges, I immediately sat down to plan. We both work so hard and I sometimes travel a lot for ministry. I learned to plan my travels and other schedules around his time. And whenever I am home during the weekend, I try to plan some exciting private time with him. With sex, I make it intentional by planning ahead - from the food we eat, what we drink and how I dress to bed.

I am very vocal when it comes to sex and making my intention known. I do not wait until he wants sex while I'm wishing or fantasizing about sex. I initiate sex and I think it makes it beautiful. The more vocal and creative you are about your sexuality to your partner, the closer you are to each other. Sex does not start from our bed but from any time that we both think about it during the day. There are times that I would have been texting my husband from work for him to get his mind prepared. And we call each other several times during the day just to keep up. Friendship makes it easy for us to get along in bed. However you can do it, be creative and ignite your intimacy.

Love can live without intimacy, but that love will not grow and deepen without the strength and glue that comes from intimacy. As a lady, you should know that intimacy improves your knowing him – from his greatest strengths to his most feared weaknesses. It is also having your good, bad, and ugly being known by him – and him doing far more than merely tolerating you. It is the two of you loving and embracing each other, in an all-encompassing way, not in spite of your weaknesses but because of them too.

Loving someone without really knowing why we do! There is something about him that holds you, possesses you; your heart is drawn to him, and while other parts of you repelled, love has a way of short-circuiting your resistance. No wonder we sometimes refer to being "in love" as being under a spell.

I think one of the real enemies of a fulfilling marriage is fatigue. The pace of life in our world today can only be classified as insane. When you are tired all the time, intimacy does not happen. Taking one night a week or once every two weeks as your night out together will be a good idea that can help your relationship. If you are too broke to get a babysitter for 2 to 3 hours, find another couple who is willing and trade kids so you can each have a date night.

From the smallest cell reaction to the most passionate emotional response, God has wired us for intimacy. God longs for you to encounter real intimacy to the depths of your being. You were made for connectedness, you will die without it. I am not talking about a physical death here but a life without intimacy spells emotional death and destruction. Real intimacy refers to the fact that intimacy is a multi-dimensional reality. It reaches beyond mere physical experience to the emotional and relational realms.

Like everything in life, our intimate relationships are subtle negotiation. They are a balance between passion and practicality, between getting and giving. Making your relationship work means juggling your needs and wants with your partner's. There has to be a clear understanding of what each person is capable of giving to the other.

By approaching life as a team, you make a pact that you will compromise along the way, while also reaping the benefits (or, as they say in investment terms, "reap the dividends") of each other's strengths.

Men and women come to adulthood unfinished and with all sorts of baggage, and over the course of a marriage they change each other profoundly. The very act of living closely together for a long time brings about inner change, not just conscious accommodation. As men and women in good marriages respond to their partners' emotional and sexual needs and wishes, they grow and influence each other.

You certainly can have a great sex life. Tell your husband what you want; tell him the right places to touch you and let him know if he is getting it right or not. Talk about lovemaking. Talk about everything. Spice up your marriage. Be intimate with your husband, because when there is intimacy, sex is just a by-product. Get information for what you don't know.

What Every Man Wants In a Woman

Now, let's get to the basics of building intimacy. What draws men and women to each other in a relationship? What etches the image of a marriage partner on the other's mind, such that wherever they are, all they can think of is being with each other as soon as possible?

Let's begin with the men. What does a typical husband want from you, as his wife? First, you must learn to look and feel good for yourself. You do not have to be reminded to take care of yourself. It is part of being responsible to take care of you. Keep what attracted you to your husband alive to keep him glued to you. Plan your schedules with your husband in mind. Do not have a schedule that will keep sapping your energy and leaving you empty to run your home. Train your children as well to be responsible. Create time for each other and do not allow another person to take your time.

Also, plan your finances properly. Do not give what you do not have; do not live for people. Live for yourself. Sometimes, the ones (extended family and friends) you are running around for are busy enjoying themselves. Why must it be you suffering and making all the money for them! Whatever time you invest affects your marriage; so, plan it well for your marriage not to suffer. And if you are a receiver, do not take the giver for granted; they have worked hard to make that money, no matter what your expectations are.

As an adult, be responsible. Do your responsibilities as a woman. Do not delegate your responsibility to a maid. Plan your home and be willing to help your spouse. This will help in sex, as sex goes beyond the act itself; it starts from earlier in the day. Know what your husband likes. Be spontaneous; be fun to each other. Be willing to learn. Be willing to teach as well, to talk about stuff. Sometimes, you may need a counselor to help you straighten out issues; at other times, you both just need to have a heart-to-heart talk. Create time for your husband and for your children, for your home as a whole. Some men complain about their wives being dirty and unkempt. You shouldn't be one of such women.

Below is a specific list of what men say they want from their wives. Please, note that the list was not written from my point of view, but from the opinions of thousands of men over a period of seventeen years, both in surveys and interviews. I asked these men to write down the top ten things they wanted in a marriage partner. So, this is an aggregate of what they said. By the way, the respondents were men between the ages of 20 to 94 years, and from all walks of life. 75% of these men attended church/mosque regularly and 30% out of the 75% were religious leaders or workers.

1. A man wants sexual fulfillment.

2. He wants a friend and an active playmate.

3. He wants an attractive/pretty wife.

4. He wants an intelligent wife.

5. He wants a woman of moral virtue.

6. He wants a committed wife.

7. He wants a wife with a sense of humor.

8. He wants a wife he can totally trust.

9. He wants admiration.

10. He wants an honest wife.

Please, take this seriously. These tips are from my notes for my Master's students (Marriage and Family). Much of this survey and interviews came from the pain, agony, and success stories of hundreds of people that I have known over a period of seventeen years as a Counselor/ Sex Therapist. They are precious people like you and me and have battled through the same crises that I have faced personally or you are now facing.

What Every Woman Wants In a Man

Really! What do women want? This was one of the most challenging surveys and interviews I ever did. I realized that what women of different age groups want from their men are not the same, unlike the men. (We are truly so complicated). Most women did not even know what they wanted from their men!

One good reason it is very difficult to understand women is because of the way women process thoughts and emotions, which is drastically different from their male counterparts. One of the key differences between men and women as I have reviewed over a period of time is that women use emotions to process thoughts as their basis for decision-making - 30% more than men do. They both use their intuition, but in different ways. Men tend to bond through shared activities but women bond through sharing thoughts and feelings.

Most women have experienced a man mysteriously closing up and withdrawing. One minute he seems available and the next he is emotionally gone. Without a doubt, it seems women generally are more interested in relationships than men, and that really is the truth. When a woman feels her man is giving less to their relationship, it is not only frustrating but depressing as well.

This note is for men about women, the woman you love, the one who loves you, the woman who drives you crazy, and the one you drive crazy. It is about what women actually want from men. After countless interviews, surveys and counseling, I was able to get the following pointers from women. Women cherish:

1. Godliness – they want a man who loves and fears God and can be the spiritual head of the home.

2. Romance - not necessarily sex.

3. Communication - they want a true friend and soul-mate who they can comfortably bare their mind to without being judged.

4. Confidence – they want a confident man, especially one that would not be threatened about thier success (leadership, independence, strength, power and self-esteem).

5. Women want men with a sense of humor (fun).

6. Women want security (responsibility/provision).

7. Women want good looks (attraction and protection).

8. Women want honesty/faithfulness.

9. Women want a sensitive and caring man/family man.

10. Women want respect.

Most importantly, every couple must realize that, for marriage to be long-term and go the distance, it must be grounded in more than a piece of paper. It requires the supernatural merging of lives and the binding of hearts. Marriage is designed to be the most sacrificial of all relationships. It is God's blueprint towards meeting our primal craving to be truly known by someone, to build a deeply committed relationship, based on honesty, trust, self-disclosure, respect, appreciation, interdependence, and togetherness. And this exactly is what God meant in Genesis 2:24, when He said, "A man shall leave his father and mother and be joined to his wife, and they shall become one flesh."

The moment you said, "I do" to each other, you were meant to leave every other person outside of your comfort and love triangle. To enjoy a marital life with fulfilling sexual bliss, you must leave everyone and everything behind and cleave with each other.

Think about what made you fall in love with your partner and talk about it. Remember the tingly feeling you had when you first became husband and wife? You thought all day about him returning home from work and your stomach did tiny flips as you gave each other a kiss or a touch. During sex, you felt like you might melt into each other's bodies and never wanted to separate. Then, fast forward to the present moment: you enjoy the deep affection you and your partner share, but the fires of your initial passion have become more of a slow burn.

Sex is about what is happening on the inside, not how we look on the outside. Maybe kids, career, or simple boredom have taken their toll. If you have found yourself asking, "How soon will it be over?" or "Not tonight again!" your relationship is probably due for a tune-up. Let's see how to go about this!

CHAPTER 4

COMMUNICATION IS KEY

"I met my husband at a dance. Several years later, it looks like I am still dancing in the dark with a total stranger.

I would love to light up the room to see this man's face, or just sit down and stop dancing, but I cannot;

So I just keep moving to the sound and pretending I am having a good time waiting for him to talk to me

And get to know me. I guess I'll just keep moving and keep dancing until I die."

—Anonymous

Many married people today live the same hollow, lonely life just like this anonymous individual. They bear a constant ache in their soul and just determine to hang on, but without hope that their spouse will change. Sadly, the woman above may have even lost touch with what it means to be a woman!

Communication is to love, what blood is to the body. When it stops flowing, the marriage dies. Communication systems allow men on earth to talk to men on the moon; yet, often, husbands cannot talk to their wives as they sit across from them at the dinner table, if at all they sit together to have dinner anymore.

Deep within each man and woman is a common longing: the desire to find comfort, companionship, and fulfillment. From what the Bible says, life is all about relationships, particularly with God and with those we love. You do not have to go very far in the Bible to see that God desires a relationship with each one of us. Even more, He is a pursuer, who works to win our hearts. His desire is for us. When His love touches us, everything changes and when we love someone, regardless of whether it is warranted or not, we are freeing ourselves to be loved as well.

The same God placed a similar relational impetus He has for us in the hearts of both men and women. God installed this for a purpose; His standard is the only perfect reflection of redeemed sexuality and a redeemed healthy union between a male and a female. The solution to conflicts in a marriage, then, is not to "keep your options open," looking for a way out; it is to press deeper into God's plan, which is to discover the true roles of man and wife in a beautifully ordered marriage. Does this sound impossible, or too difficult to achieve? I assure you, it is not an impossible goal. God can reorder your marriage. He can help you overcome criticism, hostility, disappointment and emptiness.

Looking Inwards

God's starting point is most often our own hearts. He seldom changes the circumstances before He changes us. When we find a battle going on in our marriage, the first place we should look for a solution is where our Lord starts – our own heart. When the change does begin, husband and wife will see that they do not need to spend the rest of their lives as "strangers still dancing in the dark".

Have you ever visited a foreign country where no matter how hard you tried, communication remained just beyond your grasp? You spoke as loudly as you could, you used all the sign language you could think of, and still made little or no headway in retrieving the information you needed? I remember the first time I was in Mexico, it was simply me talking without any headway for about two hours, until my host showed up. All I was telling them was, "I am the missionary you were expecting." When my host eventually showed up and told them who I was, they all embraced me, with hugs and kisses.

Similarly, seeking clear communication with your spouse can leave you feeling like a foreigner in a strange land, if you do not understand each other simple's language of love.

Are you afraid to talk to your spouse? You might be thinking, "no way"; but take a look at the way you and your spouse communicate. You might be surprised at how fears keep you apart.

Sometimes we might feel like we are walking a tightrope between being true to ourselves or to another person. We want to be independent, but we are scared of being lonely. We long to be close to our spouse and yet we do not want to be swallowed up by him or her. And the question is, how can we be individuals and yet not be left alone? We retreat into silence because it seems safer. Sometimes our attempts at communication are awkward if not downright painful.

 A man once walked into my office for counseling and revealed the most sexual frustration in his soul. But when I asked him if he had told his wife this, the instant answer I got was "No, I could never tell her that." This happens a lot, and same goes for the women! It is like we have so much to say, yet we are not saying anything. Your emotions cannot be held in check year after year without exploding. To deny your emotional feelings is disaster delayed. Holding your emotions in check is something like holding a beach ball underwater. You have to hold your breath, struggle to hold the ball beneath the water and fight furiously to keep it in check. But eventually, you will lose your grip, and the beach ball will explode and will be gone.

Communicating Right

Now, you must understand that communication is not who can yell better in an argument; nor is it the art of winning an argument. You can win an argument and lose your marriage. Communication in marriage is when your spouse can tell you how he or she feels and what he or she loves, honors, esteems, hates, fears, desires, hopes for, believes in, and is committed to, without starting "World War III". Our words are transcripts of our mind and out of the abundance of the heart, the mouth speaks.

Communication is a skill, and it is also a gift. Some of us are born better at communicating our feelings; some are built with an innate ability to de-escalate conflict, while some of us need help developing our communication skills. Communicating about your wishes and fantasies, as well as your expectations, is a window into your potential as a couple. The starting point, of course, is to understand that both sexes communicate differently.

When women want to draw closer, they face each other, lock eyes in what has been called the "anchoring gaze," and proceed to reveal their deepest hopes, worries or aspirations, their lives, and just about everything. To women, intimacy is talking face-to-face! Men, however, are somewhat the opposite, almost never looking deeply into each other's eyes. For them, intimacy is often regarded as working or playing side-by-side.

I have become accustomed to my husband retreating to his phone or the TV at the slightest opportunity. But in the early days of our relationship, it was naturally a point of frustration and contention. He fondly calls this "the cave" and, in his words, "the one part of the house that I rule." Once in there, time becomes inconsequential and the rest of the house could be on fire, with little or no regard for his attention. He would also leave the TV on as we sleep.

It was not long before I found a clever way around his solitary confinement. I personally do not like watching TV but I had to get used to watching with him, just to have the opportunity of talking to him. I've never gotten used to TV but I made it mandatory to sacrifice my time to be around him and his TV. From then on, whenever I want to have a heart-to-heart with him, all I need to do is come into his "cave" under the pretense of trying to watch too. It is a non-threatening environment for him. He enjoys narrating to me what is going on - remember this is his "cave" and he rules this world.

The purpose of this elaborate personal anecdote is to encourage you to take responsibility. If there is something in your marriage you want changed, do something about it yourself. If you find yourself withdrawing from each other, talk about it. Real communication can do wonders. What will be most satisfying is expressing individual likes, feelings, and ideas when the other person is listening attentively and the best way to get to know your spouse is by talking. Many husbands do not understand the power their words have to take their marital relationship to the next level of intimacy. In counseling women through the years, I have discovered their number one need is affirmation. We just need to hear the words that we are loved and appreciated and that our husbands still find us attractive even years into the marriage.

The Bible calls Solomon a very wise man and I agree with that. He speaks his bride's love language as he describes his love for her: "All beautiful you are, my darling; there is no flaw in you, you have stolen my heart, my sister, my bride; you have stolen my heart with one glance of your eyes How delightful is your love…. How much more pleasing is your love than wine and the fragrance than any spice. Your lips drop wetness as a honeycomb, my bride; Milk and honey are under your tongue" (Songs of Songs 4:7, 9-11).

Men can learn to affirm with meaningful words; women can learn to give their husbands the appreciation and respect they were created to receive. And when we make serving our mates the desire of our hearts, God will supernaturally fill us with His ability to fulfill that desire. We cannot properly face the task of marriage in our own strength; we must realize we need the grace of God in order to carry out even the simplest forms of communication. As we surrender our hearts and desires to His control, our communication will become a living expression of Christ's love and care.

There is something within the heart of every human being that cries out for true intimacy, and if we get it right and start speaking each other's language, we are on the right path to the intimacy we desire!

Bare Your Mind

Every couple must learn to talk to each other, even when the subject is unpleasant. The best relationships are built on trust and vulnerability. If you make efforts in making these things what they should be, the sex often follows more naturally. Sometimes, however, the sex can help get you back there – as amply revealed in the second chapter. Finding ways to keep the sparks between you and your partner requires efforts in the bedroom and outside the bedroom. It can be the hardest thing in the world to open up completely to another, but it is also the most rewarding.

Communicating about your wishes and fantasies, as well as your expectations, is a window into the potentials you have as a couple. In marriage, create your own culture. Do things that work for you. Identify what the other person wants and likes. A particular couple came for counseling and the wife's only request was for the husband to make the bed when he got up. The man was surprised that the wife could be angry about such "a little thing." And the wife on the other hand could not believe someone would get upset by asking him to make the bed. Their love life came back to life when the husband started doing that.

As individuals, we grew up from different backgrounds with different upbringings and the only way to bridge the gap is to be open about what we need and want at all times. Unless your spouse is a mind-reader, he or she does not know what you are thinking or wishing in your mind.

Discuss what you both want in marriage. Tell each other what to do to be satisfied in bed, to be satisfied in your home. When you invest in your marriage, you will definitely reap. If you still love your spouse, you should be willing to invest in it, give it all it takes. Getting involved in extra-marital affairs breeds problems for your home. Running outside cannot solve your marital problems; it will only invite trouble and sometimes destruction, not only to the marriage but your destinies and life purposes.

Forgiveness is also crucial in marriage. When the other person offends you, forgive; do not keep up piling up records of wrongdoings. As a wife, the fact that you are more financially capable than your husband does not mean you should look down on him or disrespect him. Watch out for friends whose lives are already messed up and are seeking to tamper with yours.

If you do not feel love for your spouse anymore, you can sit down and discuss, if it can be remedied or if divorce is not an option. Otherwise, if divorce is the only option after you have tried everything in your power or refused to try any longer, do it amicably without bitterness. It is better to be separated than killing each other in the marriage.

CHAPTER 5

IS SEX ALL HE THINKS OF?

(UNDERSTANDING MALE SEXUALITY)

⁓♡⁓

"The behavior of a human being in sexual matters
is often a prototype for the whole of his other
modes of reaction in life."

— **Sigmund Freud**

Sometime ago, I received a message in my email that
read:

*"I am happily married and I love my husband very much.
But he drives me crazy when he looks at other women as
they walk by on the street or in a restaurant. I feel so
embarrassed going out with him. Shouldn't he look just at
me? What's wrong with him?"*

I have equally received mails and questions bordering
on men's "insatiable" appetite for sex. Ironically, though,

there have also been a few that had to do with a husband not being as sexually active or not always making the first move, "as a man should".

Before addressing these issues relating to men's sexuality in general, let me state that we all tend to approach life with the assumption that others should see things the way we do. Among the many things to consider, one factor we often do not understand or we overlook is that how we view life is affected by our biological make-up, either as a male or a female. The way we are wired does not make us better or worse than the opposite gender; it only makes us human and unique.

When gender harmony is reached between husband and wife, it will be seen as part of God's mighty work and you praise Him. When disunity is reached instead, you might see harmony as unobtainable. We need to recognize our differences and then learn to accept them - since they do not go away. Indeed, wisdom and skills regarding gender differences are essential for any marriage to be successful and for the couple to have a fulfilling sexual life.

Engine of Masculinity

Now, with regard to male sexuality, the first place to begin is to understand that God has deposited in every man's body an "atomic bomb" called testosterone. Testosterone is the key male sex hormone and I call it the engine of masculinity because its production (often in the testicles) marks out maleness and is responsible for men's distinctive appearance and sexual development. It stimulates sperm production as well as a man's sex drive. It also helps build muscle and bone mass.

Testosterone fires a man up sexually, which is why it doesn't take much to set a man "ablaze". Men have many times the level of testosterone that women produce (yes, women produce small amounts of it in their ovaries and adrenal glands for certain biological functions). This largely explains men's heightened sex drive and tendency to be more aggressive. Men have been accused by women of being unfeeling beings but I have found that, just like women, men are inherently emotional beings. However, it takes a woman to help develop this emotional expressiveness and initiate the man into emotional intimacy.

Moreover, it is important to clarify a few other areas of men's sexuality that may be surprising to some women. First is that, just like women, men are not all the same in their sex drives. While it is true that testosterone affects men's sexuality, it is also true that certain other factors, such as temperament and age, also affect this drive. Moreover, the secretion of testosterone is not the same in every man. So, just as you may have an alpha male who is hyperactive in and out of the bedroom, so also are there men who may seem more laidback. This can be easily understood when you consider that women too do not all have the same levels of sex drive. There are indeed women whose libido (sexual desire) could be higher than that of their men. It is for each partner in a marriage to be understanding enough to see how to lovingly meet the other's needs to the best of their ability.

Second, even with the abundance of testosterone, it is not true that men want sex every time. Factors, such as allure of the wife, nature and environment of work, emotional state, as well as the atmosphere in the home can contribute to a man's desire. So, if your man seems to want sex every time, you may consider it a positive thing. It should be that he considers you really irresistible or that all is well in the home and other areas of his life.

However, just as I already noted, the fact that your man doesn't want to have sex with you every time doesn't necessarily mean that he finds you unattractive. It could, as stated above, be that his sex drive is naturally average or declining due to certain reasons, such as age or some health issues; or it could be that he is just not in the mood. Yes, despite the common belief that men are wired to be ever available for sex, it's usually hard for them to get in the mood when they are going through emotional turbulence in the home or psychological torture from work or from lack of money or from performance anxiety.

Bear it in mind also that the fact that your man has a high sex drive doesn't mean that you should not be able to occasionally turn down his sexual demands. But you must do it in such a way as not to bruise his ego. Ego is an intrinsic part of masculinity and once it is bruised, it could take a while to heal and even at that it instinctively retracts from the source of the bruising.

The third issue you should consider is that many women think sex is merely a physical thing for men and so it wouldn't matter much if they are denied. In reality, however, sex can mean much more for a man. A man could need it to feel connected to his wife, relieve stress or be rejuvenated. This can make turning down his advances as difficult for him to accept as it is for you when you are turned down. As psychotherapist, Esther Perel, says, "For men, sex is the connection. Sex is the language men use to express their tender loving vulnerable side. It is their language of intimacy."

The fourth surprising fact about male sexuality is that men want their wives too to initiate sex. They find it delightful and flattering if you can deliberately seduce them. You can do this directly or indirectly. Either way, it requires that you put yourself in the best state, physically and emotionally.

To fire up yourself and your husband for sex regularly, you must ensure to take care of any inhibitions you may have or issues bothering you. Keep the communication line open. Give your husband something to always look forward to; give him a reason to want to be with you. Give him a listening ear. Be receptive. I know you are often busy, but try to reserve some of your energy for him. Sometimes, cuddling is all that is needed; you could just snuggle up and be a blanket for him.

As a woman, learn to dress up and dress well. Sexily package your breasts; don't leave them sagging. Preferably, wear bras without wires, but that can still pack the breasts well. Try not to wear bras to bed; free your "girls" (breasts) as much as you can. Learn to have fun in your marriage. If something is not going right in your marriage, make it right. Attend classes that will enhance your sex life and your marriage. When you have issues, use what can help you feel better. Use natural products; use shea butter on your boobs. Use coconut, shea butter and olive oil for your body. Irish moss is multifunctional, containing lots of minerals needed by the body; you can take it with any meal.

Also, ensure to take care of your skin, not by bleaching your skin because it is destructive. Use products on your body that will enhance your natural complexion. Bleaching sometimes is a reflection of who the person is on the inside, it is a self-esteem issue. Don't allow peer pressure to kill you; know who you are, know the kind of friends you are willing to keep.

Fifthly, most men are concerned about satisfying their wives in bed. It's a big turn on and an ego booster for them. So don't think, when your man asks for sex, that he only wants to enjoy himself, while you just lie still. No, he needs your participation and feedback, when necessary. While it is not advisable for a man to always base his level of performance on whether his wife climaxes or not, men (at least, most) still consider it a big deal that their wives are satisfied.

Dr. Abraham Morgentaler of Men's Health Boston explains, "A lot of women can't have orgasm through penetrative intercourse, so that's not an appropriate goal. But guys want to hear from their partners that they've done a good job. If they have, then they feel good. If they get the sense that they didn't, well then, the sex was probably not so good for them. A lot of guys take their cues from women."

And of course, as already stated, if you don't feel like having sex at all, you can politely and lovingly let him know, instead of just lying there till "he gets it over with".

Checking Excesses

With particular reference to the mail I referred to at the beginning of this chapter, here was my reply:

What's wrong with your husband is that he was born a man. Men are very attracted to the physical. They're turned on by sight. When a beautiful woman who is well put together walks by a man in a restaurant, he's not thinking, "I wonder if she likes literature"; he's just drawn to her physical nature. If it's just simply looking at someone of the opposite sex and not gawking at her with lustful intention, that might require a simple rebuke to let him know how you feel about that, especially if you are with him.

We all look at people of the opposite sex every day, I might even sometimes say something like "you look cute" or "you look sharp." If course, if you are in the business world, you are inundated with such compliments. It's important that your husband knows how you feel. This is not his problem but "our problem"; so get it solved together.

I must also add that one of the struggles most married males I have interviewed have is with their in-born, hormonally – pressured interests in sex beyond marriage. These I call "sexual distraction". A husband may love his wife very dearly. He may be extremely satisfied with his sexual encounters in his marriage. But, then, when walking down the street, or in his office or just sitting on a park bench reading a magazine, or even in his own home watching the TV or surfing the internet, his thoughts turn to other women. He sees someone attractive and wonders about her sexuality. Anecdotally, at least, he undresses the woman in his imagination, and entertains fantasies of a sexual rendezvous with her. You see, this is a good man, the "I truly love my wife" type. So, he naturally wonders, "why do I have to think about women this way?"

Without any attempt to play the moral umpire, research has shown that men are morally less upright than women.

This is a fact that has nothing to do with how religious or conservative they are. If a male has been programmed with a lot of fantasy in early years, then he will continue to use fantasy as a sexual escape, no matter how satisfied he is sexually in his marriage.

To help with these issues I asked some of my conservative, religious, good men to help with a survey. About 32%, or one in three, married, morally upright and good men acknowledged that they were either extremely or strongly attracted to women other than their wives. Many are bothered by the fact that they feel attracted to pretty women!

The fact is, men notice attractive women, and they have to be blind and brain-damaged not to. No immorality is implied just because a man notices a pretty woman. However, problems come when things get deeper to attraction in a sexual way, which might lead to lust!

Men are very conscious of their propensity for lust. They are conscious of their roving eyes and feel more hypocritical than women in regard to their sexuality. Many wives know this but do not want to hear or talk about it. Women cannot understand why if their husbands really love them, they would think of other women. So, men feel misunderstood, condemned, and even despised. They withdraw into themselves and avoid sharing intimate, dark secrets that could jeopardize their marital happiness. Only 9% of respondents in my survey said they felt no sexual attraction towards other women. So, it is not his fault; that is the way he is wired.

Sexual Expectations

Wives and husbands know they react differently to sexual drive and stimulation and that their sex drives vary, but they do not understand the intricacies of their two very different systems. Yet, lack of knowledge about techniques is only one kind of ignorance. Another has to do with expectations. Below is a note from a concerned husband:

Dear Dr. B:

My wife and I have fallen into a pattern of having sex once a week—mostly on Sunday nights. She insisted it has to be at night, this suits her fine because she is a schedule-oriented person. I do not feel that she really wants to have sex but merely another item on her to-do list for the week. I try so hard to understand that this is just who she is, but I am beginning to resent her.

My response:

Try writing a letter to your wife, expressing your love and desire to be a thoughtful husband. Point out the things you appreciate about her. Then let her know about your hurt and frustration – even how awkward you feel about telling her that. Then express how you really feel about this issue.

Discuss male sexuality in general, and then mention how you feel about being controlled in your sexual interaction. Indicate you are longing to discover a more spontaneous solution for achieving oneness with her. Open, vulnerable, straight talk about your feelings and desires is the only way to avoid sounding critical or being forced to beg. While you resent this path toward sexual intimacy, your wife may be unhappy about other issues, such as emotional intimacy. Sex for sex's sake is not very appealing to a woman. But sex as the natural outcome of relational intimacy is very appealing. As the two of you talk openly, you may discover a better way toward mutual satisfaction.

Of all the areas of tension in marital sexuality, frequency of sex is the most troublesome. How often, or rather the regularity of sex in a marriage can be filled with emotional baggage, such as anger, guilt, fear, jealousy, and shame. Emotions such as anger, guilt, and shame affect a woman's sexual response more than they do a man's, perhaps because a woman opens herself to being penetrated. Becoming vulnerable is hard to do when a woman is in emotional turmoil. So how often is it to have sex? You decide! My suggestion, however, is that if you are struggling with differences in your sex drives then keep working toward sexual oneness. Sexual oneness is a process but it is worth working for because it can bring satisfaction into every level of your marriage.

A good relationship is one in which both husband and wife learn to give in to the other at times, despite what they may want as individuals. Authentic marital sexuality can be achieved only if the two are in agreement about their sexual interaction. There is no room for the misguided view that the husband initiates and dominates while the wife submits in obedience. Rather, 1 Corinthians 7:4-5 and Ephesians 5:21 assume mutual desire for an interest in lovemaking. This requires sensitive communication between the couple about their sexual desires. Just as an orchestra plays "with one voice" when each instrument contributes its own unique part and the music is brought together in harmony, so a married couple reaches sexual harmony through communication and sensitive understanding of each other's needs.

Having a good relationship with each other is among the most difficult tasks there is. It means you are looking at yourself honestly, while trying to join with another. A loving relationship has to be an ongoing negotiation. It is not a battle for control or a one-way street, in which one partner is getting his or her needs met while the other is not. There has to be a clear understanding of what each person is capable of giving to the other. By approaching life as a team, you make a pact that will compromise along the way, while also reaping the benefits of each other's strengths. Like everything in life, our intimate relationships are a subtle negotiation. They are a balance between passion and practicality, between getting and giving. Making your relationship work means juggling your needs and wants with your partner's. It takes two to do the job!

Remember, good sex never starts in bed. Instead, marital sexuality should include an element of playfulness. Although playing games with one another's emotions is destructive, a sexual relationship benefits from a sense of fun and playful interaction, which depend on an absence of self-consciousness or embarrassment about nudity and sexual involvement. Honesty in communication, a healthy view of oneself and one's body, and comfortableness with one's partner are vital ingredients of being free to bring playfulness into a sexual encounter. Accordingly, the level of fun in a relationship is often a good measure of the degree of intimacy. When two unite and truly become one, both should feel enveloped in love, security, respect, and trust. An understanding of the differences between a man and a woman is the first step to a healthy sex life.

Is mutual sexual satisfaction really possible for every couple? Yes—and you as a man can make the difference! God designed sex to be a vital, passionate expression of marriage. Your wife is a very complicated creature – emotionally, hormonally, spiritually, relationally, and sexually. Her variety and intensity may appear in the sexual realm as unpredictability and strong reactions – both of which can intimidate and confuse you. To deny the multiple facets of womanhood is to reduce her to a single dimension—the sex object!

Is it wrong to look at other women?

Here is another letter I got from a worried husband:

I am happily married but sometimes when I look at other women, I get aroused. It just happens. Is that wrong? How long is too long to look at a woman, I know the Bible talks about lusting in your heart, I just do not understand.

My Opinion:

It is certainly a normal male physiological response to be aroused by seeing an attractive woman. Short of having some serious, disfiguring surgery to rid you of sight, that tendency may continue into old age! Lol…. But here is the real issue: What does a guy do in response to visual arousal? That is where lust begins but you can overcome that.

"Wow, didn't God do well when He designed women?" That might be a better expression when you look at an attractive woman. Instead of lusting, you can just acknowledge and remember that your spouse is God's gift to you and look away. I just personally feel sorry for men these days with all these unwanted flesh that is out there but you can control it if you want. That may include walking away, or changing channels if you are watching the TV.

The sense of unity and fulfillment that is so essential to a successful marriage is not destroyed by a single act or event. It erodes gradually in small, barely discernible ways. Only after months or years do you realize how far you have drifted apart. You might think you are happily married but personally I think you do not have a fulfilled marriage. If you are truly in love with your spouse and everything is going on well between you two, I do not think another woman can arouse you by just looking!

CHAPTER 6

HER AMAZING BODY IS MADE FOR LOVE

(UNDERSTANDING FEMALE SEXUALITY)

$\heartsuit$

"Sex pleasure in woman is a kind of magic spell; it demands complete abandon; if words or movements oppose the magic of caresses, the spell is broken."

—Simone de Beauvoir

It is true that biology, as well as experience and learning, has shaped men and women to view sex talks, acts and lovemaking somewhat differently. Some say it is because we are brought up in distinctly different ways, almost as though we live in separate cultures – sometimes almost separate planets. In my experience, men and women often speak in negative generalizations about each other. Men often say that women are engulfing, sexually unresponsive, too sensitive, moody, and very absorbed in personal appearance. And women often say that men are unemotional, condescending, and thoughtless of other people's needs.

Sex is the ultimate expression of the body and every woman has the right to a satisfying, electric, passion-filled sex life. I mean, everything you have always dreamed of and more. You just have to believe it to make it happen. And the beginning of the solution is our bodies. Learning about your body, and awakening and relishing its potential, is every woman's starting point for a healthy, confident sexuality. Too many women are strangers in their own bodies and it is not surprising. I see it in the women I work with all the time. Communication about sex is missing or even discouraged in many women's lives, making their foundation more than a little flimsy for the bumpy journey that sex inevitably is!

Some of our parents tried to do their best in our formative years, but whether it was because they felt uncomfortable or uninformed themselves, they often failed to give us the information we needed and craved for at the time. When it was given, it was sometimes laced with negative judgments.

The messages from the media and the society often come with "good girls do not…" The truth, however, is that sex is power and this is why I seek to bring awareness and rediscovery to women on the path to sexual wholeness. This way, the focus shifts to exploring and finding ways to bridge the fundamental difference in the ways that men and women approach sex. In the end, it's the coming together that makes sex the sweetest.

Like many parts of life, women need to feel their way through sex. There will be pain and ecstasy along the way, soul-mating and sometimes "heart-breaking". But the journey is what makes the woman – in life and in love. The thought of sex stirs up all kinds of feelings: desire and need, excitement and anxiety, nostalgia and fantasy. A woman's sexuality is ultimately a combination of the experiences she has already had, along with the untapped potential that still lies within her. Past relationships, childhood experiences, and her own unique personality – all collide to create the female sexual identity. Since the phase of our lives is always changing, our sexual needs are constantly in flux as well.

Hormonal Activity

Hormones play a vital role in your sexual response and are critical in sexual function. Without them, not much would be happening in either your brain or your genitals. From a physiological standpoint, there are two essentials for great sex: balanced hormones and good blood flow. These generally depend upon good health. While a woman's sexual anatomy and response play the leading role, the rest of her body acts as the supporting cast. Many health conditions and medications that have nothing to do with sex can have a noticeable impact on your sex life nonetheless. Women must learn to recognize and treat the health challenges that crop up over the course of a lifetime to keep their sexual response functioning smoothly, too.

The sex hormones – estrogen, progesterone, and testosterone – affect sexual desire and arousal throughout the course of a woman's lifetime. Testosterone is a fundamental source of sexual energy for women and men alike. Estrogen helps keep the vagina lubricated and flexible, which is essential for comfortable sex. It also increases serotonin activity in the brain, which is associated with better mood, more energy, and improved memory. When your estrogen levels are too low, the vaginal tissues begin to thin and weaken and you may experience vaginal dryness. The most common result is painful sex. This is a time to get a lubricant to do the job for you; they are handy and available in flavors now and on the counter in the drug stores (reach out to me if you do not understand what this is).

For men, the process is fairly simple – though not always so, as we've seen in the previous chapter. They have a fairly consistent level of testosterone, which affects their sex drive, as well as their sperm production, hair growth, muscle mass, and aggressiveness. A woman's hormones are more complicated. Estrogen levels are typically at their lowest during perimenopause, after menopause and childbirth, especially if you are breastfeeding. While estrogen levels will return to normal in women who have recently given birth after they stop breastfeeding, menopausal women undergo a permanent reduction when the ovaries stop functioning. The ebb and flow of hormones affect a woman's moods, vascular system, breast, bone health, skin, hair, vaginal mucosa – and sexual receptivity. No wonder women are so fascinating - and so difficult to predict.

In my own words, if you have stopped childbearing, are not thinking of a career and are between the ages of 35 and 50, then those are your prime years to enjoy sex the most. You only live once; you do not want to look back and say I wish I'd had more sex. Have a great sex life!

Take Charge of Your Satisfaction!

Good sex does not just happen, but you can make it happen by listening to your body. You are the authority on what your body needs and wants. Society is not your authority, neither are magazines or even books. Medical doctors can help, if you know you have a medical problem, but they cannot know what your body is telling you. Neither can your husband. You can discover with your husband what you enjoy and communicate that to him. Do not expect him to know how long or how hard or where or in what order you like to be touched. Take responsibility to know and tell him how you would like to make love; he cannot read your mind!

How do you learn to listen to your body? You begin to pay attention to the messages it gives. You respect the signals and take them seriously. You may notice your desire as an urge for closeness and touch. You might feel edgy as an indication of your need for release, or you may experience genital sensations.

Listen to your body during the sexual experience too. However, listening and paying attention to your body's signal is not the same as watching. Monitoring how you are doing will get in the way of your body's experience. Sex works best when you get lost in enjoying each other and satisfying the hunger inside you – not when you keep a close track of your body or your husband's responses. Watching creates self-consciousness and interrupts pleasure. Become an active player. You cannot watch and play at the same time!

As a man, if you believe your masculinity depends on your wife's responses, you are headed for trouble. Since a woman's sexuality is unpredictable, relying on her desire for you is not a great way to build the security that lets intimacy grow. When your self-worth rests on your ability to sexually fulfill your wife, you will both feel pressured to achieve that goal. As already stated, a woman's sexual enjoyment is naturally fulfilling to a man, but a focus on getting her response in order to validate you will decrease pleasure for both of you. It can destroy passion, as well as intimacy.

Power of Communication and Consideration

Regardless of the complexities of a woman's sexuality, I believe that a high level of understanding and mastery can be attained by a couple through thoughtfulness and communication. This means that even though a woman is in the best position to know what works for her at every point in time, a truly loving husband would still be mindful of making every sexual experience an exciting one for both of them. This involves seeking to know what she finds most pleasurable.

Below is a mail I received from a concerned wife and the response I gave is a clear pointer to how female sexuality can be maximized for mutual satisfaction.

Dear Dr. B,

My husband is really gentle and loving, but he also thinks he understands exactly what I want in lovemaking. It's like he does not believe me when I say something else would feel better or arouse me more. What do you recommend?

My Response:

You have taken a great first step in communicating your sexual likes and dislikes to your husband. But you may need to try new ways of communicating. You know your husband better than anyone, so listen to the way he talks, and try to use ideas that he's most familiar with. Keeping the discussion light, you might try a direct challenge. You say your husband is really loving and gentle, then go ahead and tell him what turns you on. He will want to listen and please you.

Men and women have different approaches, expectations, and hormonal drives for sex. Men usually want more frequent sex and greater variety in sexual play. Women usually want more emotional connection through conversation and tender touch. They also prefer more consistent lovemaking techniques. These difficulties can lead to tension over positions for intercourse, frequency of sex, and experimentation with different sources of stimulation. But differences can also provide a great opportunity to develop mutual submissiveness as each partner looks for ways to show love to the other.

If a sexual activity does not bring both of you enjoyment, repeating it eventually causes resentment. Self-focused sex often involves power or control. Sex becomes an invasive, dominating behavior that violates the personal dignity of another person. God wants us to enjoy the passion and pleasure of lovemaking. Some boundaries were established to protect and enhance the maximum enjoyment of the gift. One is that both of you agree on what you do to find enjoyment and pleasure in lovemaking. When you assume that you know what the other is thinking, feeling, or wanting, you might be wrong. And do not assume that the other knows what you want either, you can do much and better when you talk about it. For a healthy sex life, tell each other what you like or do not like in sex. Whatever you do, do not assume anything.

Essential to a satisfactory sexual relationship is an atmosphere of mutual caring, friendliness, openness, sharing of feelings, and commitment. There must be mutual tolerance for shortcomings, a spirit of forgiveness, mutual concern, trust, and freedom from fear. In short, there must be love. Without love, sex has the potential to become a monster. Good sex gives us something to look forward to in the daily grind of our lives. It matters for our minds, our bodies, and our relationships. By carving out a space for it when life seems overwhelming, we make sexual pleasure a priority again. Sometimes, women simply need to learn that it's ok to put themselves first. The bedroom is a great place to start!

CHAPTER 7

SPICING UP YOUR SEX LIFE

"Anyone who is in love is making love the whole time, even when they're not. When two bodies meet, it is just the cup overflowing."

— Paul Coelho

Sex is the fiber of your relationship with your spouse. It is the act that distinguishes you from roommates and offers a way of uniquely revealing yourselves to each other. At its best, sex is a channel for communication and connection between the two of you. At its worst, sex is a chore that begins to feel like a mere echo of the pleasure you once shared. When you got married, emotions ran high as you explored and savored each other. As real life inevitably intrudes on your relationship, it is essential to find ways to tune back to those days when everything was exciting. Both partners need to feel satisfied with what is going on in the bedroom. It is important to make it work for the two of you and compromise is the key.

Let's look at the various techniques you can adopt to fire up your sex life again.

Setting the Mood

The foundation of fulfilling lovemaking, as has been emphasized throughout this book, is to purposely create an atmosphere of love, trust, respect, harmony and thoughtfulness in your home on a daily basis. It is to ensure that you and your spouse are emotionally connected at every point in time. With this in place, it becomes easy for every other "trick" you apply to work.

That being said, let's get to the specifics. Lovemaking can be either spontaneous (can happen anytime or begin anywhere in the house) or pre-planned. Either way is fine, depending on your feelings and the prevailing circumstances.

Now, the most effective way to put your spouse in the mood for sex is to profusely speak their love language. Love languages fall into five categories – words of affirmation, acts of service, receiving gifts, quality time, and physical touch. Each of these is important and expresses love in its own way. You should therefore, learn your partner's, as this communicates love to them clearer than any other thing you may do. Here is a wife's experience, for example:

"On our wedding anniversary I came home from grocery shopping and he had cleaned the bathroom and kitchen from top to bottom and that meant more than anything else he bought me or did for me for our anniversary this year. It also indicated to me that he wanted to spend time with me when I came home, because he knew I would have to do that before I could relax with him."

Did you notice that she clearly emphasized that the service he rendered was by far more important to her than anything else he bought or did? This means that if he had just limited himself to buying gifts for her, it might not have put her in the mood!

Other ways you can put your spouse in the mood and also let them know you are in the mood is by dropping hints, teasing them sexily, sending flirty messages to them while they are away, touching them playfully (some grab or spank their spouse's butts, as they walk by), specially preparing the bedroom, lighting candles or dimming the lights, playing music that sets them on fire (have a sexy playlist on standby), spraying some cologne, slipping into the shower with them, putting on a sexy new bra and panties (as a wife) or simply waiting in the bedroom for him stark naked and so forth.

Note however that what puts each individual in the mood is not always the same. For instance, there are people who seem to find it difficult getting hints; they consider it much sexier for someone to communicate their sexual needs to them directly – not like a command but like a deep longing, such as "Honey, I need to make sweet love to you tonight." Yes, sometimes, you have to go radical to make your man or woman go bananas!

Now, that we have set the mood, let's see the next important element.

Roles of Foreplay

Foreplay encompasses a range of activities that a couple engages in before the actual sex (penetration), with the purpose of getting fully aroused and achieving maximum pleasure. Such activities include hugging, fondling, caressing, undressing, kissing, petting, nibbling and even whispering sexy words into each other's ears.

Foreplay helps to prepare both the mind and the body for sex. This means that, without it, sex may not be fully enjoyable and could, in fact, be very painful. Women, in particular, need good foreplay to be fully aroused in preparation for orgasm. As someone said, when it comes to sex, men are like microwaves, while women are like slow cookers. In other words, most women don't get turned on by the flip of a switch; usually, it takes some stage-setting and, dare I say, strategy.

Foreplay prepares your body for sex by causing an increase in your heart rate, pulse, and blood pressure;

dilation of your blood vessels and genitals; increased blood flow to the genitals, which causes the labia, clitoris, and penis to swell; swelling of the breasts and erect nipples; as well as fully lubricating of the vagina, which can make intercourse more enjoyable and prevent pain. So, don't just go straight for penetration. Allow both of your bodies to give the signals of being fully ready to be "devoured."

However, as already indicated, the mind also has to be put into a good state through foreplay. This, again, is more important for women. When a man gives adequate time and attention to exploring a woman's body before going for full-blown sex, it communicates to her that you really desire her and that you are also interested in pleasuring her to the fullest. This, in itself, is a powerful turn on for sex!

Erogenous Zones (Sexual Hotspots!)

To have a mind-blowing foreplay and deeply satisfying sex, you need to be familiar with the erogenous zones of the body of the typical male or female, and especially the body of your own spouse. An erogenous zone is an area of the human body that is extremely sensitive, which, when stimulated, can cause heightened sexual arousal and orgasm. While there are basic sexual organs almost everyone is aware of, the truth is that individuals experience different levels of sensitivity with these organs. And what's more, there are other parts of the body that many do not pay attention to but are very sensitive, and could in fact, be the exact places that your spouse wants stimulated for his or her arousal.

Typical erogenous zones for men include the penis, the mouth and lips, the scrotum, the neck, the nipples, the perineum (the area between the anus and scrotum), the ears, the bellybutton, the back of the knees, the nape of the neck and the lower back. For women, they include the clitoris, the vagina, the breasts and nipples, the mouth and lips, the nape of the neck and collarbone, the ears (especially the ear lobes), the pubic mound, the inner thighs, the stomach (especially the navel), the butt, the upper and lower back, and the center of the chest.

There are three important things you should note about these sexual hotspots. One, as already said, it's up to you to join your spouse in exploring and discovering which works for you best. Second, even though these are the most sensitive spots, you make sex more enjoyable if you don't go for them first. You can begin with other parts of the body before going for them. This is a form of teasing and serves to heighten anticipation and desire from your spouse, such that when the zones are eventually stimulated, they are ready to explode! So, make sure you savor every part of your spouse's body, and not just these zones. You may even discover more as you explore further!

The third important fact is that these zones are not just helpful for foreplay; they also contribute to reaching climax or orgasm – the very peak of sexual pleasure! So, even after actual penetration is on, don't stop stimulating these super sensitive zones. Continue, as much as you can, and your spouse will definitely appreciate you for it!

Mood Killers

Well, life is full of opposites. So, since there are sex mood enhancers to try, there are also mood killers to avoid, before, during and after sex.

Turn-offs for Women

- Poor hygiene

- Bad breath or body odor

- Untrimmed pubic hair

- Body shaming

- Excessive roughness with sex or fondling

- Lack of creativity

- Looking at the phone

- Asking, "Are you there yet?"

- Not knowing when to stop

- Stopping immediately after ejaculating and rolling over to sleep

Turn-offs for Men

- Poor hygiene

- Drab undies

- Insisting on lights off during sex

- Being silent or motionless

- Unwillingness to experiment

- Being too clingy – holding so tight that the man can't do much moving

- Faking pleasure

- Looking at the phone

- Talking too much

- Too much drama

CHAPTER 8

TACKLING SEXUAL PROBLEMS

A sexual problem is one having to do with sexual desire or response and it could manifest in many forms. In men, sexual problems often come in form of erectile dysfunction (ED) and premature or delayed ejaculation. For women, sexual problems may include spasms of the vagina, vaginal dryness and pain with sexual intercourse.

Men over 65 years of age are at a higher risk for ED, although ED is not a normal part of aging. Among women with sexual problems, 43% say decreased sexual desire is their primary challenge. The problem for both sexes may be psychological, physical, or a combination of both. Though there are many causes of diminished libido and sexual dysfunction in men and women, there are also many ways to increase libido and rekindle the joy of sex once you identify the problem.

When sex is turned into an obligation, there is no way it can be enjoyed. As earlier stated, upbringing can affect a person's outlook to sex. A man completely lost interest in sex because of what he saw while growing up. The father would bring home different women and would beat up the mother. This made him lose interest in marital relationship. He got married late and the wife cheated on him. This made him lose whatever interest he had left in sex. Such a man would need multiple counseling and therapy sessions to get back on track.

Now, let's go into the details of sexual problems.

Sexual Problems in Women

Sexual problems in women are grouped into different disorders: sexual pain, problems with desire, arousal problems, and orgasm difficulty. Changes in hormone levels, medical conditions, and other factors can contribute to low libido and other forms of sexual dysfunction in women.

Specifically, sexual dysfunction in women may be due to:

- **Vaginal dryness:** This can lead to low libido and problems with arousal and desire, as sex can be painful when the vagina is not properly lubricated. Vaginal dryness can result from hormonal changes that occur during and after menopause or while breastfeeding. Psychological issues, like anxiety about sex, can also cause vaginal dryness. Anticipation of painful intercourse due to vaginal dryness may, in turn, decrease a woman's desire for sex.

- **Low libido:** Lack of sexual desire can also be caused by lower levels of the estrogen hormone. Indeed, different factors could be responsible for low libido in women; stress is a major factor and anti-depressants drugs don't help much. Emotional and mental issues are a great factor as well, when it comes to sex. Also responsible for low sex drive in women is menopause; women's low libido and sex drive decreases as menopause comes upon them. So, how do you deal with menopause? You need to know when exactly menopause is occurring. If your periods cease, go check up what it is in the hospital and don't just draw a conclusion that it is menopause.

- **Difficulty achieving orgasm:** Orgasm disorders, such as delayed orgasm or inability to have one at all, can affect both men and women. Again, some antidepressant medications can also cause these problems.

- **Pain during sex:** Pain is sometimes from a known cause, such as vaginal dryness or endometriosis. But sometimes the cause of painful sex is elusive. Known as vulvodynia or vulvar vestibulitis, experts do not know what is behind this mysterious type of chronic pain during intercourse. A burning sensation may accompany pain during sex.

All couples should be able to enjoy a healthy sex life — an important part of a relationship. If you are experiencing any sexual problem, get in touch with your doctor. You can often correct your problem by:

- Getting an accurate diagnosis and the proper treatment of any underlying medical condition

- Talking to your partner openly about your sexual relationship

- Avoiding alcohol, smoking, and drug use

- Managing stress, anxiety, and depression

- Getting creative and re-energizing your sexual routine

- Good communication can unlock closed doors in the bedroom; so start by talking to your partner about physical and emotional intimacy. And, if you suspect a medical condition, talk to your doctor about what could be going on with your body.

Sexual Problems in Men

The types of sexual problems men may experience include:

- Erectile dysfunction (ED): ED can be caused by medical conditions, such as diabetes or high blood pressure, or by anxiety about having sex.

Depression, fatigue, and stress can also contribute to erectile dysfunction.

- Ejaculation problems: These include premature ejaculation (ejaculation that occurs too early during intercourse) and the inability to ejaculate at all. Causes include medications, like some antidepressants, anxiety about sex, a history of sexual trauma (such as a partner being unfaithful), and strict religious beliefs.

- Low Libido: Psychological issues like stress and depression, as well as anxiety about having sex also can lead to a decreased or no sexual desire. Decreased hormone levels (particularly if testosterone is low), physical illnesses, and medication side effects may also diminish libido in men.

Generally, for men, sexual dysfunction can be temporary or long-lasting. The causes vary and may include:

- Being age 65 or over in men
- Childhood sexual abuse
- Taking certain prescription medications, including some antidepressants
- Hormonal imbalances
- Drug abuse
- Depression, anxiety, or other psychological and emotional issues

- Stressful life events
- Certain medical conditions, such as diabetes, coronary heart disease, high blood pressure, arthritis, and sleep apnea
- Vaginal infections
- Injury, such as pelvic fracture

What to Expect at Your Health Provider's Office

Your doctor will do a physical examination. Many times, laboratory tests and a physical exam may not show a cause. Your doctor may ask about your ethnic, cultural, religious, and social background, which can influence your sexual desires, expectations, and attitudes. Your doctor may test your hormone levels, particularly levels of testosterone, which affects sex drive in both men and women.

Treatment Options

If depression is causing sexual dysfunction, my advice as a holistic practitioner is to deal with the root cause of your depression. Therapy is a great tool to use; so, get a Counselor that can help your situation. I do not personally campaign for antidepressants because as a practitioner, I know that the side-effects are damaging to your health. Most antidepressants may cause low libido, others may not.

Erectile dysfunction – Some medications can treat erectile dysfunction, but may have potentially serious side effects in some men. Again, as a holistic practitioner, I advise you to use alternative medicine to treat your issues. It is not an overnight healing or magical therapy but it will gradually reset your body back to the right place.

Problems related to menopause - When estrogen levels drop after menopause, women may have vaginal dryness and other changes that may make sex painful. Women who have painful intercourse after menopause may want to ask their doctors about the available therapy, as a vaginal ring or cream. Over-the-counter products are available as creams or gels for women who have vaginal dryness.

Finally, note that a variety of psychological, behavioral, and interpersonal therapies may also help with sexual disorders. For example, combination therapy, including both sex therapy and alternative medicines, may work best for all dysfunctions.

At FemFis Wellness, it is our passion to help you with the best alternative medicines and therapy. Reach out for our free consultation.

CONCLUSION: LOVE UNCONDITIONALLY

Lovemaking is a blessing given by God. Enjoy it. If there are issues, sit down and find a solution. To keep your marriage strong and sizzling, you and your spouse must learn to respect each other, be able to sit down and discuss issues, however big or small. If you cannot do that, then you need to re-check your marriage. Avoid drifting apart; this can be achieved when the communication line is kept open. Consciously plan your marriage, and determine to make it failure-proof.

Here are some action steps you can take:

- Have a vision for your marriage because without a vision, there is less reason to make the relationship work. "Where there is no vision, the people perish", says the Bible.

- Make deposits into your love bank, nurture your relationship every single day.

- Are you a giver or just a receiver? Don't be at the receiving end only, learn to give as well.

- Go to your foundation, if need be. Do what needs to be done. If both of you need to shed weight, do it together. You need to invest in yourself to be healthy. Pay attention to yourself and take care of yourself. A woman could have hormonal imbalance that could lead to weight gain, treat it.

- Learn submission to each other. Some things you fight over are not worth it. Ephesians 5:25 says a husband should love the wife as Christ loves the church; men ought to love their wives in this manner. Your wife needs to know you love her, and then submission becomes an easy thing, you won't need to fight it. Love, respect and humility are all reciprocal. As a wife, respect your husband; respect makes your husband long for you, it makes him desire you.

I believe strongly that the most important decision you will ever make is whether or not you receive Jesus Christ as Savior which will determine the quality of life you live on earth and the eternal life you will have in heaven (this is from my Christian belief). I recently attended Easter service at church and the title of the message was "Jesus at the Center." I could not stop writing - I kept on going, and worship was excellent. I attend an international church with people from all over the world. My Pastor is Caucasian but he does not see the color of the skin, and when he preached that particular sermon, I understood perfectly why he does not see the color. He is such a humble man with a heart for Jesus.

It is all about Christ, my dear friend. When He is at the center of your heart, you love unconditionally! When Jesus is at the center of your life, you love out loud and in resilience. Jesus was not a religious leader; His message was love. He only ministered for three years yet He remains the most controversial. He broke the ice by breaking the rules and the odds. He obeyed the laws of the land but broke the laws of the Pharisees (the hypocrites.) He loved, in spite of the law; He broke the barriers and touched the untouchables. He ministered to the women and He ate with them. He loved unconditionally and He gave His life in the process. He was crucified for saying the truth and for loving the weak. He is a God of grace and of mercy, He loves you, despite your shortcomings.

Jesus is my role model; He is at the center of my heart. He dominates me and controls me; He navigates my moves, my thoughts and my entire being. He leads and I follow, and since I surrendered it all some years ago. I am a better person. I reason better, I think well. I think deeply and ask, what would Jesus have done? When people talk to me or treat me in a certain way now, I know I am not their problem, something must be wrong in their soul and I love them instead.

Life is better when Jesus is at the center. It does not matter if you have been a Christian since birth, re-examine your life and see if your actions and your thoughts are centered on Jesus. When you make Jesus the center of your life, you are a changed person. You see differently and love unconditionally. Your life should be expanded and take a new meaning. Stop being a Pharisee; embrace Jesus and renew your thoughts and your actions. Be free because the truth will set you free and you will be happy.

I want you to know that Jesus is no more on the cross. He rose from the grave. He is risen, He lives and He reigns forever! I have just one question for you, my friend: Is Jesus at the center of your heart?

Pray thus:

Lord, I rededicate my heart right here before you. I place my whole life in Your hands. Fear has no hold on my soul anymore because your blood has broken the chain. I called and You answered and came to my rescue. I just want to be where You are now, God. Be lifted higher in my life, in my love and in my world. Amen